Foreword by the author Charlotte del Rio

A story of truth in a rescue sanctuary 112 Carlota Galgos of a galgo's dream for her forever
Based upon love and dedication my heart tells the tale of abandoned souls who long for their Christmas wish. A forever home

Can Santa and the fairy galga grant the wishes of the orchard galgos?

I wish to thank you for purchasing this book and helping us to continue our work with the plight of the Spanish Galgo. Education is paramount to us and the future of the galgos. With your help change can come!

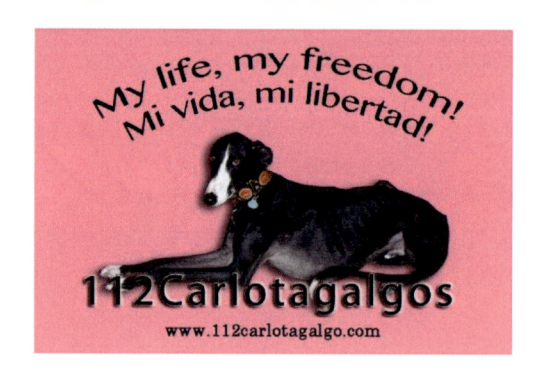

A Galgo's Christmas Wish © 2014
Charlotte del Rio
comdelrio@hotmail.com
www.112CarlotaGalgos.com

A *Galgo's Christmas Wish*

Written by Charlotte del Rio

With gratitude to Simone Carline Carter (known as the artist Nellie Doodles) who has provided the artwork

Thank you to Eli Galga who has assisted with the publication of this book

112 Carlota Galgos was set up in 2006 by Charlotte and her family

It is based in Malaga, Spain

112 Carlota Galgos is now an association which rescues as many galgos as possible

Charlotte is supported by her husband Dioni, and children Neizan, Sofia and Sebastian

The Children of 112 Carlota Galgos

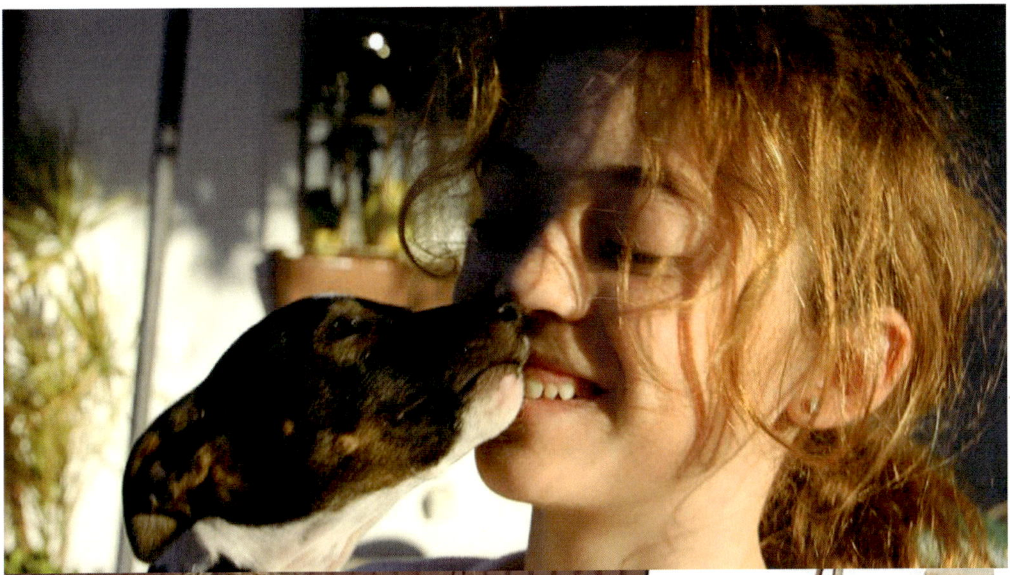

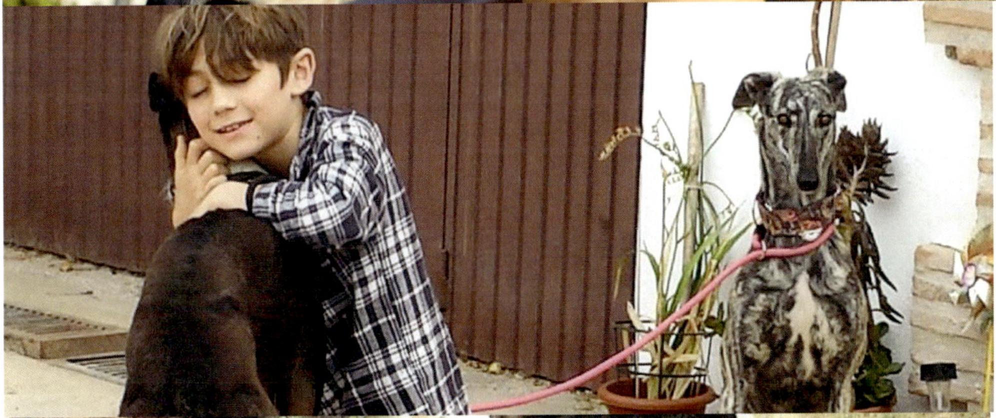

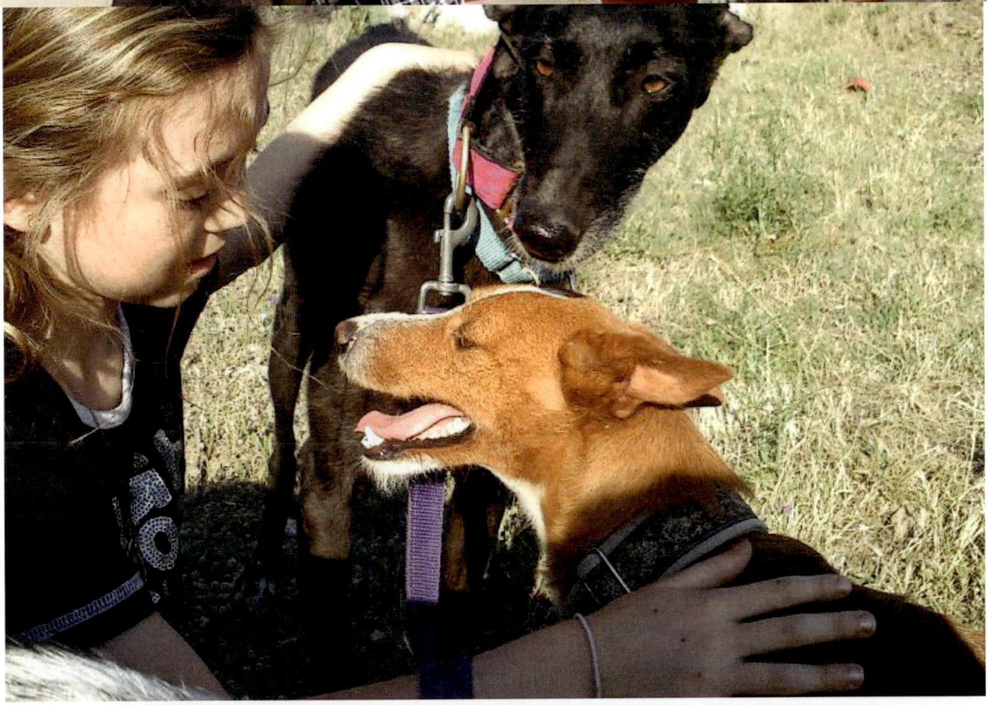

Our Galgos are ready to tell you their

Christmas Story

A Galgo's Christmas Wish

It was the night before Christmas at Finca 112 Carlota Galgos. The peace which oozed at the finca coupled with the childrens excitement was astonishing. As the sounds played from the box on the wall which Charl calls the radio, tunes of Merry Christmas played. All in preparation for the BIG man's arrival!

Neizan had been telling the galgos all about the man who comes down the chimney dressed in red and bearing gifts for all the good boys and girls. "Including the galgos" he went on to say.

"Well, just who is this man?" asked Pinkie to Happy. "You're wise and older…. Can you tell me?" "No sunshine, I can't….No one ever came to me before. No red man….No white beard. Just a big man with heavy boots. Steel capped toed that really hurt when I got the boot." "Ooohh" said Pinkie…."Nooo, that's not what Neizan said of the man in red!" "No" lil galga Hazel commented…"Oohh, goodie goodie," says lil baby Olivia……"well just who is he then?" Hazel began……"Sit down my loves and I'll tell you a story…….Once upon a time I saw the sky light up in the dark.

Sprinkles came down upon me and the whoosh of angels led the way of his huge carriage sleigh….." "What's a sleigh Hazel? What's a sleigh?" "Oohhh Magenta, it is royal and big and is drawn in the night by a special animal who lights the way." "Ahhh", she said "Wow! Woof Woof!" Lady jumps up all interested. "Tell us more Hazel. For I never saw this before!"

"I looked up at that star filled night and it was cold. Colder than cold. There he was, dancing through the sky….. and saying 'Ho Ho Hooooo!' Merry Christmas one and all." "What does that mean wise galga?" chirps up Leo. "Well, it's a day of miracles when a special baby was born. The humans celebrate this miraculous birth and give gifts and eat a lot."

"Ahhhh that never happened to me" says Geo. "Never."

"I fell to sleep on the eve of what's called Christmas to wake up to a shower of gifts. Bones, and it rained down miracles. The magic filled the air and all I'd wished for was that my nose didn't leak and my body was warm. To my surprise the glitter came washing over me….. the magical air, the gifts fell at my feet, bones, food, blankets to keep me warm. More than I'd asked for, and as I looked up the big red man saluted me"

"Ohhhh wow!" says Zoe. "Me, me, meee, I'd like to see him too" "Meeee 3!!" says Poppy. "Have we been good?" says Amber.

Leo chirps up "Look who's coming through the gates……
Ask Charl! She always says we have been good. Here
she comes…..But Oh! What's wrong? She wears a
frown. Ohhh, our Charl"

"Well kids" Hazel says, "Charl's shoulders are heavy, Adina
a new galga reminds her of Prince. She's been rescued
and Charl wears the worry. Ya see these beds? The filled
bowls? The blankets? The man who makes us feel better
when we're sick, Paco…It comes at a cost.

For the humans, Christmas is a very busy time for families. But as Charl says, WE are her family and they are our family….we spend it together. She never leaves us" "WOW" says Zoe……"Gosh……She's sad!...Run everyone!....All paws on Charl!!!!" "Wait, wait" says Hazel. "One thing you must know is that when Charl says its bedtime, you must go to bed. No messing. PJ's on….Dinner all gone….or the big man won't come" "Oh we will, wise Hazel. We promise" says Olivia. "But hey Hazel" says Duke. "What does Charl ask the man in red for?" "Ahhh…" says Hazel. "Space for us all" she says… A finca, forever love

A place so that when we've gone home, there's a way to carry on. Food, blankets and love. That's what I heard Neizan say…he held her hand and said "One day mama…..the galgos will be safe forever! A place for the children to come. The educational centre will be born". Like baby Jesus….No matter her fears, her worries…..She never tells us. She sings to us and smiles! That's right…She puts our world right! That's what Christmas means. The gift of giving…The finca gives so much to us all and those before us and those to come. Give thanks little ones…OK, go now…Run…Paws on Charl."

"Oh how they run, wise Hazel" says Leo. "Yes Leo…The young have had enough torture, it won't hurt for them to believe their paw prayers will be answered. Their homes prepared and that they will sleep next year by their own families' chimneys…"

Leo asks "No one ever visited me, You Hazel, for real?" As Hazel turns, her head lowers… "No Leo. The night the magic came it was what they call frozen water. Snow embraced my body and I dreamt of all I have now. A bed, food and love. A kind hand filled with courage and softness yet strength that I knew I was safe. Charl says my day will come and I will need to say goodbye to her. But for my own family and my own chimney to guard… No, my friend….that night, the only man who visited me was in my dreams. When I woke to my master's boot…I knew it was a dream.."

Hazel walked off to her bed in Jade's house. The galga with wings they call her by tribute. Charl wears her in her heart as many do.

Leo looked and watched and caught up with the gang. The blankets that Charl carried were thrown in the air….Happy hugs all around. "I'm far too independent for hugs!" Leo thought. "But it sure is nice to feel love….".
Night fell and all were in bed. Charl gave each galgo their nightly tuck up and kiss. Neizan, Sofia, Sebastian and Dioni came down to wish all a Merry Christmas Eve.

Lights out, the music played….

Closing eyes, the galgos fell asleep. Olivia one eye peeping slowly gave way to sleep. As the night passed Hazel sighed. Another year gone…..

As the night was crisp, in the distance she heard "Ho! Ho! Hooooo….! Woof! Woof! Woof!...!" A twitch of the ear and shake of her head…Hazel thought she was dreaming again.

To her surprise, through the window of Jade's house, she saw THE most wonderful sight she had ever seen. For there she was….this white and grey galga. The galga with wings sooo large with every flutter!! The man in red laughing his "Ho Ho Ho!" as his sleigh went high and low. Hazel's heart began to flutter… Blinking once! Twice! Three times! Shaking her head…Goodness! It's real….HE is real! JADE is real…! On each feather she flaps away the worries of all and lands with the sleigh in the orchard.

Wow….tears fall from Hazel's eyes at the pure serenity of this stunning galga with a message for all…. "There's a home for you all! A Forever! Santa" she calls…."This orchard's special" He sees the house of his fellow friend and knows. He nods! Woooosh….Off they go in a second and the magic air is filled with excitement.

As dawn comes the household's up. In steps the family. All joyous to share their love. Hazel began to stir. She shook her head in disbelief….did she…..was she….had she been here? The galga with the huge angel wings with grace and pureness as Angels come. Had she seen the man with the sleigh and bells?

Lil Olivia jumped out of bed…"Zoe Zoe wake up its Chrissssssstmas." "Ooh joy" says Poppy. Not sure what to expect. All doors swing open….yeehaw everyones out bombing round the orchard. "Yes yes yes look all" says Lady…..theres a big black bag on the gate of Jade's house.

Wow running they tear it apart. Treats Food And Toys for all. "Ooooh wow he came" says Olivia.

In the form of Dioni thought Hazel quietly.

As the gang tucked in to Christmas Gifts wise old Hazel lay down on a comfy bed wishing others a comfy bed. She lays her head down.

To her surprise Charl's not here. Why-ever not? She's always here! Oh well. Dioni walks past and caresses her head. It's all OK Hazel.

Nei says "Wow you must have all been good". He sees twinkle dust on the ground and wonders…."huh what's this? I wonder" as Geo smells the ground.

"Whoaaaa what's that? "chirps up Victor. Its Charl she's squealing……uh oh What's wrong? She comes racing round the corner to the orchard full speed ahead like a galgo. "Well she's had plenty practise" jokes Lady.

"Hazel" she shouts over joyed. "HAZEL HAZEL….. Its here he came for you……HE DID NOT FORSAKE YOU. HE DID NOT FORGET YOU"

Hazel all shy at the mass attention coils in her bed and taps her eye. Ever the Lady thought Leo.

"Hazel, this came for us at the base of our chimney. Let me read it to you….Sit down…. We, dear Hazel are on our way. We're flying high and you're coming to stay. For this is just the very start, for you have stolen our very hearts. We, your family will be there soon…..And all your past will be removed. Love Mama and Papa xxx". The tears fell that day from Charl's cheeks. "A real Mama for you Hazel! No matter what…. The Christmas spirits real. For life on earth is about giving and loving"

Hazel coy at the news breathed in the air. The spirit of Christmas and she knew what she saw in the night sky was real. As real as Charl sitting next to her.

Thank you Jade she felt in her heart….thank you

Proud as anything Charl hugged her Hazel. Merry Christmas Hazel my love. Merry Christmas one and all xxx

There were 14 Galgos in our Magical Christmas Story one extra! Do you know which galgo If you are not sure the answer

Pinkie

Happy

Leo

Geo

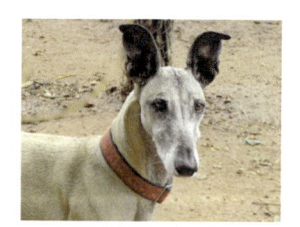

Hazel

Zoe

Lady

Olivia

Below are the photos of these beautiful Galgos with below was not in our Christmas Story?
can be found at the bottom of this page

Poppy

Amber

Adina

Victor

Triumph

Duke

Magenta

25

Answer: Triumph

Ambo

The Ambassadog of 112 Carlota Galgos

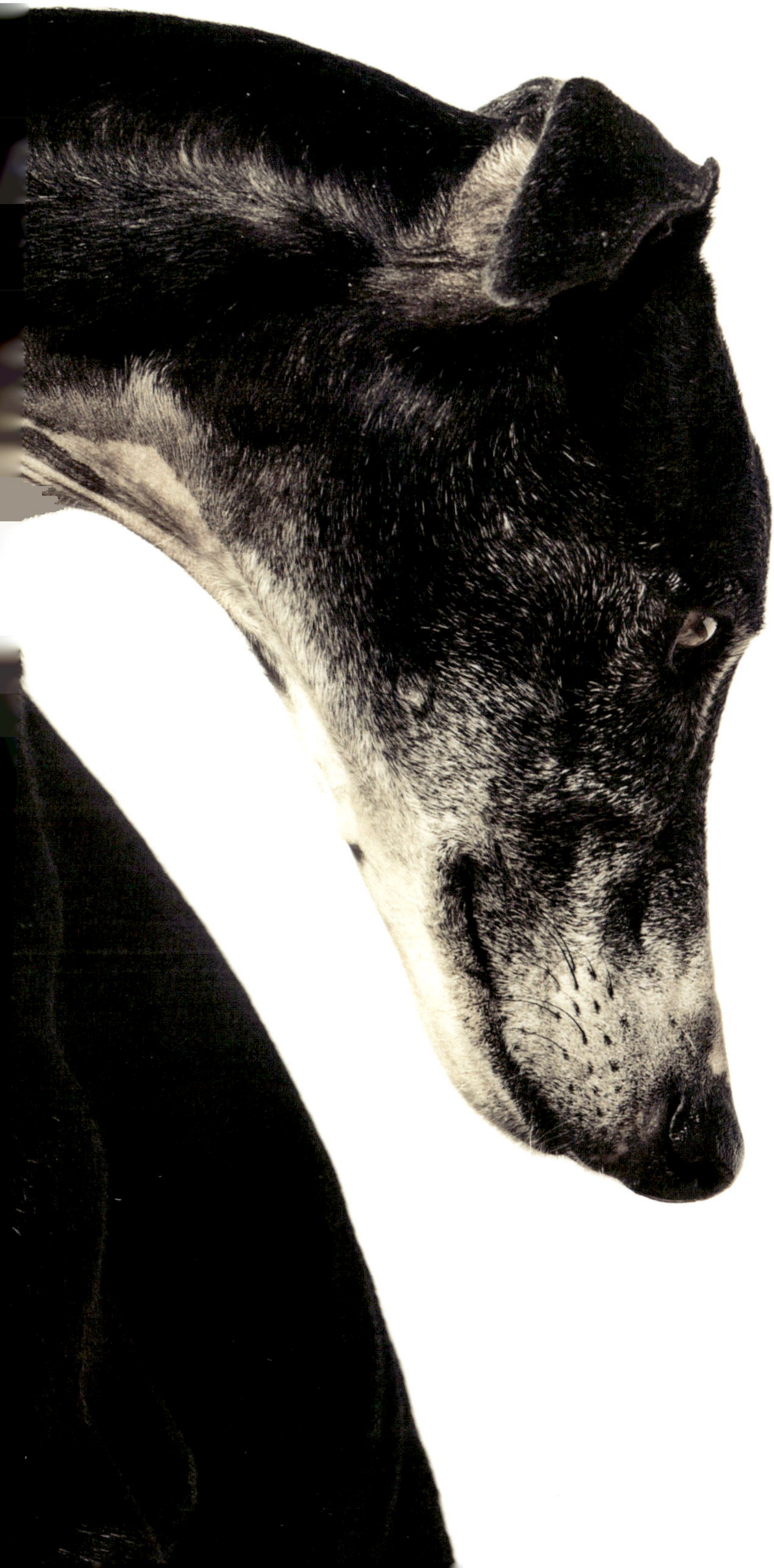